Christmas Time with Teddy Horsley

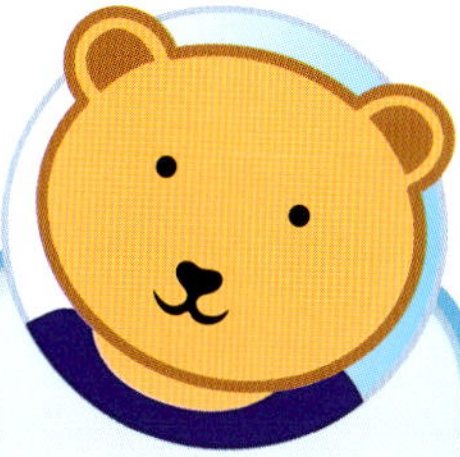

Leslie J. Francis and Nicola M. Slee

CWR

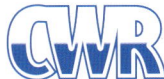

The Bear facts

Teddy Horsley and Betsy Bear are part of a churchgoing family. They live with Lucy, Walter, and Mr and Mrs Henry. The Teddy Horsley books are designed to build bridges between the young child's day-to-day experiences of the world and major biblical themes and stories. The series is a result of extensive research into the religious development of young children, and the authors' wide experience of educational work in schools and churches.

Both authors work in church-related institutions of education. Nicola Slee is a freelance writer and educator based at Queen's College, Birmingham. Leslie J. Francis is Director of the Welsh National Centre for Religious Education and Professor of Practical Theology at University of Wales, Bangor.

Published 2005 by CWR, Waverley Abbey House, Waverley Lane, Farnham, Surrey GU9 8EP, England.

See back of book for list of National Distributors.

Concept development, editing, design and production by CWR.

Printed in China by 1010 Printing International Ltd.

ISBN 1-85345-357-9

Other titles featuring Teddy Horsley and Betsy Bear published by Christian Education, include:

It is Christmas Day and Teddy Horsley is a very excited bear.

Teddy Horsley gets dressed and goes out
with Lucy, Walter and Betsy Bear to hear the
Christmas story.

Mr and Mrs Henry lead Teddy Horsley past the shops and Christmas trees until they come to the church.

Inside the church, Teddy Horsley and Betsy Bear meet with their friends to take part in the Christmas play.

They choose costumes to become shepherds and kings, angels and innkeepers, Mary and Joseph.

The story all began when the Angel Gabriel
visited Mary and brought her news of great joy.

'Do not be afraid,' said the angel to Mary.
'You will have a baby boy and name Him Jesus.'

The story all began when the angel of the Lord
visited Joseph and brought him news of great joy.

'Do not be afraid,' said the angel to Joseph.
'You will marry Mary and take care of her
Son Jesus.'

The story developed when Joseph and Mary made the long journey from Nazareth to Bethlehem.

Joseph and Mary went to an inn to find a comfortable place to stay and somewhere safe for their baby to be born.

The story developed when the innkeeper turned Mary and Joseph away to find shelter in a cattle shed.

That night the baby Jesus was born and placed in the cattle's feeding trough, while the animals looked on.

The story was proclaimed to the world when the shepherds looked away from their sheep and gazed up into the night sky.

The angels shouted aloud that the Son of God had been born in Bethlehem and told the shepherds to go and see.

The story was seen to be true when the shepherds followed the dusty road to Bethlehem and found the cattle shed.

The shepherds went in and discovered it all as the angels had said, seeing Mary, Joseph, and the baby Jesus.

The story was proclaimed to the world when the
wise men looked away from their camels and
gazed up into the night sky.

The bright star in the sky shouted aloud that the King of kings had been born in Judea and told the wise men to go and see.

The story was seen to be true when the wise men followed the star and came to the place where Jesus was.

The wise men went in and found it all as the prophets foretold, seeing Jesus, Son of God and King of kings.

The story found its response then in the hearts of people when the wise men knelt and presented their gifts to Jesus.

They placed at Jesus' feet the gold of kings, the frankincense of priests and the myrrh of ordinary people.

The story finds its response now in the hearts of
people who kneel at Jesus' feet today and offer
themselves to Him.

Teddy Horsley and Betsy Bear join with the people of God in bringing their gifts to celebrate Jesus' birth.

It is Christmas Day and Teddy Horsley is a very excited bear.

There were some shepherds in that part of the country who were spending the night in the fields, taking care of their flocks. An angel of the Lord appeared to them, and the glory of the Lord shone over them. They were terribly afraid, but the angel said to them, 'Don't be afraid! I am here with good news for you, which will bring great joy to all the people. This very day in David's town your Saviour was born – Christ the Lord! And this is what will prove it to you: you will find a baby wrapped in strips of cloth and lying in a manger.'

Suddenly a great army of heaven's angels appeared with the angel, singing praises to God:

'Glory to God in the highest heaven,
and peace on earth to those with whom he is pleased!'

When the angels went away from them back into heaven, the shepherds said to one another, 'Let's go to Bethlehem and see this thing that has happened, which the Lord has told us.'

So they hurried off and found Mary and Joseph and saw the baby lying in the manger.

Luke 2:8–16

These questions suggest further ways of developing links between the young child's experience, the story and the Bible passage.

Talk about Christmas:

Where have you seen Christmas decorations?
What have you seen in shops?
What have you seen in streets?
What have you seen in churches?
Have you seen images of Jesus?

Talk about Christmas cards:

What have you seen on Christmas cards?
Have you seen pictures of Jesus, Mary, Joseph?
Have you seen pictures of shepherds, wise men, angels?

Talk about the story:

Who brought news to Mary?
Where was Jesus born?
How did the shepherds find out about Jesus?
How did the wise men find out about Jesus?
What did the wise men give to Jesus?

Think some more about the story:

Who would you want to be in the play?
What would you like to give to Jesus?
When will you go to church at Christmas?

National Distributors

UK: (and countries not listed below)
CWR, Waverley Abbey House, Waverley Lane, Farnham, Surrey GU9 8EP. Tel: (01252) 784700 Outside UK +44 1252 784700

AUSTRALIA: CMC Australasia, PO Box 519, Belmont, Victoria 3216. Tel: (03) 5241 3288

CANADA: Cook Communications Ministries, PO Box 98, 55 Woodslee Avenue, Paris, Ontario. Tel: 1800 263 2664

GHANA: Challenge Enterprises of Ghana, PO Box 5723, Accra. Tel: (021) 222437/223249 Fax: (021) 226227

HONG KONG: Cross Communications Ltd, 1/F, 562A Nathan Road, Kowloon. Tel: 2780 1188 Fax: 2770 6229

INDIA: Crystal Communications, 10-3-18/4/1, East Marredpalli, Secunderabad – 500026, Andhra Pradesh.
Tel/Fax: (040) 27737145

KENYA: Keswick Books and Gifts Ltd, PO Box 10242, Nairobi. Tel: (02) 331692/226047 Fax: (02) 728557

MALAYSIA: Salvation Book Centre (M) Sdn Bhd, 23 Jalan SS 2/64, 47300 Petaling Jaya, Selangor.
Tel: (03) 78766411/78766797 Fax: (03) 78757066/78756360

NEW ZEALAND: CMC Australasia, PO Box 36015, Lower Hutt. Tel: 0800 449 408 Fax: 0800 449 049

NIGERIA: FBFM, Helen Baugh House, 96 St Finbarr's College Road, Akoka, Lagos. Tel: (01) 7747429/4700218/825775/827264

PHILIPPINES: OMF Literature Inc, 776 Boni Avenue, Mandaluyong City. Tel: (02) 531 2183 Fax: (02) 531 1960

SINGAPORE: Armour Publishing Pte Ltd, Block 203A Henderson Road, 11–06 Henderson Industrial Park, Singapore 159546.
Tel: 6 276 9976 Fax: 6 276 7564

SOUTH AFRICA: Struik Christian Books, 80 MacKenzie Street, PO Box 1144, Cape Town 8000.
Tel: (021) 462 4360 Fax: (021) 461 3612

SRI LANKA: Christombu Books, 27 Hospital Street, Colombo 1. Tel: (01) 433142/328909

TANZANIA: CLC Christian Book Centre, PO Box 1384, Mkwepu Street, Dar es Salaam. Tel/Fax: (022) 2119439

USA: Cook Communications Ministries, PO Box 98, 55 Woodslee Avenue, Paris, Ontario, Canada. Tel: 1800 263 2664

ZIMBABWE: Word of Life Books, Shop 4, Memorial Building, 35 S Machel Avenue, Harare. Tel: (04) 781305 Fax: (04) 774739

For email addresses, visit the CWR website: www.cwr.org.uk

CWR is a registered charity – number 294387

These titles published by **Christian Education**

www.christianeducation.org.uk

A Teddy Horsley Book
The Sunny Morning
Teddy Horsley celebrates the new life of Easter

A Teddy Horsley Book
The Broken Leg
Teddy Horsley meets Jesus in all who help him

A Teddy Horsley Book
The Windy Day
Teddy Horsley and the Holy Spirit

A Teddy Horsley Book
The Present
Betsy Bear meets the Three Men